# POEMS THAT DON'T WIN PRIZES

Poet Liz Hicklin has been waxing lyrical since her parents sent her to elocution lessons at the age of five. Encouraged to entertain guests before the days of television, and being the daughter of a pontificating Methodist lay preacher, she embraces the power of the podium. Avoiding the profound, she prefers to put pen to paper when the spirit moves. She writes short stories and has published a selection of poetry books; a true story, Limerence, published 2021; and her memoir, Kiss and Cry, in 2023. She has performed on the ABC radio, in the United States and the UK, and just about anywhere she is offered a gig.

# Poems that Don't Win Prizes

LIZ HICKLIN

*TABLE OF CONTENTS*

4 POEMS THAT WIN PRIZES
6 MY TULIPS
8 ON WRITING POETRY
9 EVENSONG
10 THE BRIDAL SHOWER
11 PAIN
12 WARNING
13 NIGHT NURSE
14 AUSTRALIA
15 THE TROUBLE WITH POETS
16 HEARD ON LEAVING A POETRY CLASS
17 ON READING THE BOOK 'FURY' by KATHERINE HEYMAN
18 THE QUICK RED BROWN FOX
20 YOUNG ALF GRATTIDGE - MY FATHER
22 PLAGUE, MARCH 2020
24 HOPE IN DIFFICULT TIMES, AUGUST 2020
25 THE FLOWER STEALER
26 A POEM FOR TED HUGHES
28 LOVE IN THE RETIREMENT VILLAGE
31 FOG
32 THE PILL
34 THE DOLLMAKING MAN
37 PINE NUTS

38 MORNINGTON MADNESS
40 THE NATURE OF POETRY
42 TODAY'S WORLD
44 OLD LADIES AND THEIR DOGS
46 ADAPTION —A SLAM POEM
48 WAR GAMES
50 THE KISS
51 SILENCE
52 MOTHERS BEACH, MORNINGTON
53 THE ICE QUEEN
54 TONI
56 THE PRIVILEGE OF AGE
57 ASSISTED
58 TO LIZZY
60 FAMILY GATHERING

# POEMS THAT WIN PRIZES

*On reading the winners of the Peter Porter Prize.*

Poems that win prizes
don't make sense.
to me.
They must have resonated
with the judges,
who must
be on a higher intellectual plain
than myself.
I will never be a prize winner,
I need to make sense,
at least to myself.

What is a prize-winning poem anyway?
The seizing of words
shot into the air,
with meaning only
to the perpetrator.
Spare me!
Intellectual gobbledegook.

# MY TULIPS

You carried me through the lockdown.
Brown bulbs I buried months ago,
waited and watched, even forgot.
Eventually
you peeped. I'm excited.
Green shoots became bold,
growing confident, asserting yourself.
Clasped tightly, keeping the secret hidden.
Then it appeared, a hint of orange,
turning into a vibrant flaming ball,
an upright phallus
watered and watched.
You didn't disappoint.
Then, your neighbour appeared.
Blood Red, look at me, look at me!
I did.

For days, superlative and supreme,
like confident chorus girls,
you filled my heart with joy.
Today, the music is waning
as sex-ravaged maidens,
your petals all asunder
like a drunken opera singer
on a triumphant note
in love with the tenor,
capitulate.
I'm yours!

# ON WRITING POETRY

When writing poetry, one bares one's soul.
To be derided, admired or ignored.
Poetry is the delicacy of words,
woven, assiduously chosen.
Poets are surgeons of the tongue,
They delight in reading their own work,
Sharing with like-minded people.
Poets are unique - aren't we?

# EVENSONG

I sit at night in my window
and watch the sun-setting sky.
The flickering lights across the bay
bring to mind the Great Gatsby
and a lover across the water.
I read poetry then, the poetry of others.
It sooths my soul.
The red sky shrieks,
'Look at me, my last moments!'
I do—I'm mesmerised.
You tantalise me with your glory,
but you won't stay—
it wouldn't be right.
Blackness hangs there patiently.
It's all choreographed:
the thin red line shrinks,
blackness is threatening now.
You slide, to give
the other side of the world,
your indulgence.

# THE BRIDAL SHOWER

The bridal registry rejoices.
Bridesmaids
lithe, long-legged ladies
mingle with myriads of marauding maidens.
Recognising relatives reverberating.
Garrulous Grandmothers gesticulating.
Animated Aunts anticipating.
The cutest of Cousins contemplating distant dreams.
All to pay homage to the beautiful bride-to-be.

# PAIN

Pain is a person,
standing outside oneself.
To be considered,
humoured, reckoned with,
as only the sufferers know.
'Are you ready for bed?'
I enquired of my friend,
Particularly prone to that person.
'Not yet,' she replied,
'I can't lie down,
until the orchestras died down.'

# WARNING

Time hangs heavy in a junkie's hands.
Ghostly pale and whippet thin,
Blackened fangs and gentle grin,
Some mother's darling boy.
Better be killed in a filthy war,
Than led to your death by this gentle whore.
For one will give you a hero's end,
The other, you'll die without a friend.
Beware, all ye who through these portals glide,
Only the very strong survive.

# NIGHT NURSE

As if growing old wasn't enough,
The added burden of broken bones.
Delicate frames worn thin with the years,
Worn weary with wearing and ready to break.
Some minds gone, by way of escape.
Each lady, my mother, all over again.
Twelve thousand miles, when she needed me most.
A wrong I never can rectify.

# AUSTRALIA

They scoured the heavens for months, years.
The odd titillating woolly cloud mocked.
The parched earth cracked, capitulated.
They prayed, implored, yearned for rain,
It came.
Mercilessly, the heavens opened, as if by punishment.
Water churned relentlessly,
crashing through dumb-struck dams.
People clambered for safety.
The moon looked down mockingly
on the receding waters.
Five hundred thousand cattle sacrificed
to the God of Rain.

# THE TROUBLE WITH POETS

The trouble with poets is
we like to be heard.
Scattering our words of wisdom
among the proletariat.
We would be wise to observe.
Before we speak, ask ourselves,
Is it necessary?
Does it improve silence?

# HEARD ON LEAVING A POETRY CLASS

To be a poet
does one have to be mentally deranged?
No, not certifiable,
but bordering on the strange.

# ON READING THE BOOK 'FURY' by KATHERINE HEYMAN

Instill me with your intensity,
your mastery of words.
You make
my eyes stick out like beacons.
It's harrowing,
stunning.
You leave me speechless.
I will still be me when I've finished your book,
But -- a little of you may have seeped through.

# THE QUICK RED BROWN FOX

There was chaos in the bush block, turmoil heralding the dawn,
Four whippets on the wood pile, sniffing, snarling with the morn.
With gun in hand I prodded, and out shot a lightening streak:
The ruddy fox who ate my chicks — guts full, he'd been asleep.
Four dogs took off in hot pursuit, their prey they pounced upon,
And then began the deadly dance, a limb for everyone.
Around they waltzed in silence, feet that scarcely touched the ground.

With gun I stood, but powerless, then came the gurgling sound.
The fox's mouth chomped one pup's head—I'm stunned and mesmerised,
but beat the beast, its jaws of death relinquishing the prize.
The limping pup retreated, and the fox, whose blood-shot eyes
Gaze into mine appealingly, I saw truth that never lies.
My fatal blow released him, letting go his mortal coil --
Extinguished and defeated, his brutal life I'd foiled.
Now the dogs play unabated, with no thoughts of yesterday,
But that fox's eye will haunt me until my dying day.

# YOUNG ALF GRATTIDGE - MY FATHER

Ran a marathon
out of the Manchester slums.
He had ambitions.
World War One made him a captain,
fighting on the Somme.
He never mentioned the war
but there was an army greatcoat in the wardrobe.
He came home to his sweetheart Nellie,
four babies, two of each.
He exported Manchester textiles,
worked hard, mentally and physically.

The Methodist church beckoned,
'Beatlemania' of the day.
Sunday saw him pontificating from the pulpit --
'The Power of the Podium'
he passed on to me!
Each child settled in a different country.
He was proud.
Mother not so.
She lived with a bag full of photographs .

# PLAGUE, MARCH 2020

Fire, flood and pestilence.
All three in just three months.
Smug in our once-thought complacency,
our vulnerability laid bare,
this will test our resilience.
Who would have thought,
that a creature simple as a bat
could bring the World to its knees?
No need for firearms in this war --
brains are what are needed.

The enemy is invisible,
selective, leaves no prisoners.
Basic precautions our only defence.
Each individual responsible.
Healthy lungs a positive,
damaged ones may succumb.
Scientists the world over
work to conquer.
We wait, to be a statistic?
(Or not.)

# HOPE IN DIFFICULT TIMES, AUGUST 2020

There is hope,
of a vaccine on the horizon.
Hundreds of busy people
gazing through microscopes,
working to conquer
man over matter.
What brought the world to its knees
may yet be extinguished.
Meanwhile, the earth rests.
We rest.
Will we resume normality
wiser?

# THE FLOWER STEALER

She operates mainly at dusk,
private property no deterrent.
It's the bloom.
She's mesmerised.
It's involuntary.
With breathtaking creativity
she weaves her magic
producing
the perfectly prettiest perfumed posy.
I'm envious.

# A POEM FOR TED HUGHES

A flippant girl bent on boys and laughter,
You stopped me in mid-air.
Trapped in your fantasy
Birds, wind and animals.
Words.
Choking in wonder
You led me headlong into literature.
I left, eager for the World's wonder.
Still clinging to the thought of you.
Led crying to my bed on your marriage.

Public libraries and book shops chorus your name.
My children studied your works.
Memories sit silent twelve thousand miles between.
Your misfortunes screamed headline news.
Mine make gutter journalists grovel.
Personal hell makes good copy.
To walk on a wind-swept moor,
Shed like a lizard the bad parts,
Blown to obscurity.
Hope and innocence remain.

# LOVE IN THE RETIREMENT VILLAGE

She announced that she would marry
Even though he's 82.
He was tall and quite good looking,
Slim and charming too.
Her kids looked on in horror,
Predicting future woes.
'But I've been a widow ten long years,
With another ten to go.'
So they joined in holy wedlock,
Sealed their union with a kiss,
With high tea at Brooklands,
They entered married bliss.
But as the days grew longer,
Harmony was not quite right.
The only thing that bugged her,
Was, his enormous appetite.
His breakfast was gigantic,

She thought he was a nutter.
Cornflakes, muesli, juice and two boiled eggs.
Slices four of toast and butter.
Each dinner was a marathon,
She hadn't cooked for years.
Let alone peel all the vegies
She was nightly close to tears.
Cabbage, carrots, beans and broccoli
He nightly placed before her,
She'd known he had a garden,
Hadn't dreamed that it would floor her.
One night she said, 'My dearest,
I married you for better and for worse.
But I find my darling,
These vegies are a curse.
I hadn't realized sweetheart,
When I blithely said 'I Will',

That it gave me charge of your large tum,
My nightly task to fill.
You see dear, things are changing,
Heard of Women's liberation?
No longer are we slaves to men,
There's been a transformation.
I pledge to love you darling,
Play scrabble every night.
I'll even let you share my bed,
When the temperature is right.
So, peel your own potatoes,
Shred the cabbage and the beans,
I'll play with my computer,
Whilst you're working up a steam.'

# FOG

*Manchester 1946*
Cherry-nosed, teeth-chattering children
pour out of school
plunge into thick, dense, frightening fog.
As we crawl past rows
of smoke-belching chimney pots,
gloved hands reach out to clutch fellow siblings,
terrified that the Gypsies down the lane
might spirit us away.
Years later, as I lie on Elwood beach,
the sun pours down from the bluest of blue skies.
Pity the people of Manchester
do not know that the sky is not always grey.
That's how it was before climate change.
I believe now they even have barbeques!

# THE PILL

My granddaughters.
It saved our lives,
but it has ruined yours.
Well, not quite,
just certain aspects of it.
The ultimate jewel in the crown.
To fuck, or not to fuck?
The longing,
the anticipation,
the expectation,
After much soul searching,
the final surrender.
Then.
Nights of worrying.
Oh No-----

Count the pence.
Knock twice and ask for Mary.
Just in time,
thank God, that little spot of blood.
Saved once more.
Now, it is just a matter of course.
Online meeting.
Nice body.
All boxes ticked.
Off we go.
Marks out of ten
What did you say your name was?
Your star sign?
See you on Facebook.

# THE DOLLMAKING MAN

For months now I've been waiting.
Not sexually discriminating
To have a mere male undertake,
The task, a porcelain doll to make.
Monsieurs, Jumeau and Kestner,
Both male, none the less for,
Ran the factories long ago,
From whence the dolls did flow.
Today's male, hung-up and macho
No way would you catch-o,
Me, making a doll
You can't call me a Dolly Troll!
With intrepid consternation,
Geoffrey joined the operation.
Deftly gently did he take,
Dream Baby in his hands to make.
Like a craftsman tried and true,

Each stage he laboured through,
Identifying by degrees,
Painting lashes, stuffing knees.
His body was a masterpiece,
He held it up with pride
Stuffed 'ard like a soccer ball,
Firm and tough inside.
'Now, let's complete the little fella,
By giving him a M-A-M-A.'
Geoff felt that inappropriate,
As it wasn't saying P-A-P-A.
Though I've solved the problem,
But I only caused a howler,
By suggesting rather tactfully,
'Let's insert a Teddy Growler.'
Must admit, I laid it on a bit,
When giving him advice,
On sewing for the little mite,
And how to make things nice.

'Remember, only cotton lace,
Buttons, loops the like,
Mind, no synthetics –
Make it right.'
And when the dress was finished,
He showed it off, right proud.
Been 'eavy 'anded with the spray starch,
It was stiff, just like a shroud.
It was as if God sent,
This poor unsuspecting lamb,
Retribution for indignities,
Caused at the hand of man.
Male Gynaecologists, Hairdressers,
A mincing round my chair,
We're in their hands so often,
One had walked into my lair.
And because the modern feminists,
Worked hard to make us free,
I just suggest occasionally,
'Geoff, your turn to make the tea!'

# PINE NUTS

The view from my window is rooftops, concrete paths.
Today, the white cockatoos are vying for position
on the tall and slender, perfectly formed,
Pencil Pines.
They jostle, push each other away
feathers fly,
Who will be 'King of the Castle.'
They have discovered the pine nuts,
A carpet of white, breakfasting on the green verge.
With hooked beaks and clawed feet,
they delicately feast on the delectable nut.
Spilling out onto the road
oblivious of danger,
carelessly discarding the husks
I drive to the supermarket to buy my pine- nuts
in a plastic bag.
a delicacy
labour- intensive
expensive.
I use sparingly.

# MORNINGTON MADNESS

(Written pre-virus)
Main street awakes, swishing sweepers sound,
Adidas pumps daily pounding the ground.
Dog owners next, precious poodles parading,
Market folks set up for a busy day trading.
Fanatical swimmers head straight for the sand.
Eggs freely ranged.
Local honey farmed.
Up and down the shoppers go,
No thought of Michelangelo.
Dress racks screech 'Nothing over 20'.
Plums and peaches in this land of plenty.
Broccoli, celery, crunchy and green,
The lusciousest lettuces you've ever seen.
Bacon, eggs, kransky, on hot plates sizzling,

Tired toddlers in arms, restless and grizzling.
6pm comes, pull down all the shutters.
'Time for dinner', the old ones mutter.
Retiring retirees retire at 8.30.
Town springs to life once again at 10.30.
Shivering Sheilas in neck-plunging minis,
Laconic boys, their arms full of tinnies.
The oldies dream on of passions long spent,
Youth's only worry is paying the rent.
Italian waiters through aisles duck and weave,
'I'll have one with the lot, please, and dripping with cheese.'
The world keeps on spinning this merry-go-round.
We're so lucky to live in this great sea-side town.

# THE NATURE OF POETRY

The poetical brain,
is hard to explain.
Comes out of the blue,
forms of various hue.
Takes one by surprise,
some days when you rise.
Might come from a dream,
an unusual theme.
Whatever, it's unstoppable,
most likely improbable.
Friends turn away mystified,
who cares, you are satisfied.
Does it come from the heart,
does it come from the soul?
Whatever its source,
the words just unfold.

It brings you such calm,
can't possibly harm.
When I am on my poetry planet,
just leave me alone, damn it.
My ego's at play,
it's lightening my day.
My brain's all awhirl,
got to give it a twirl.
But this rhyme is so trite,
among literary giants.
Where do I stand?
Repressed, or defiant?
Unable to tweet,
rhymes eloquent, sweet.
I will never reach fame.
I'm a down-to-earth Dame.

# TODAY'S WORLD

Do we question or dare,
When we're led by despair.
We were raised with ideals,
That were truthful and real.
But the world closes in,
Dominated by sin.
Multinationals rule,
We learn that at school.
This world of technology,
Quite free from theology.
Wide open to scammers,
Without any manners.
Young and old in their power,
As we learn every hour,
They strip your identity,

Without any empathy.
eBay's so alluring
And quite reassuring.
Buy this, it's so pretty,
Turns out to be shitty.
Refunding improbable
Human contact impossible.
Put it down to experience,
You resolve to have diligence.
What happened to Grace?
Everything's so 'in your face'.
Wellness, Yoga, Meditation,
But there's always medication,
To get us through life,
In this world full of strife.

# OLD LADIES AND THEIR DOGS

They are everywhere these days,
Old ladies with their dogs.
They walk their little darlings,
In rain, in shine, and fogs.
They love their little pooches,
Take them walkies in the park,
But when mother goes a shopping,
When left alone they bark.
For the owner, its incredulous,
I left her with a bone.
That's over in a minute,
It's you she wants at home.

Take heed you poochy people
When you cuddle every night
They cannot live without you,
They can't bear you out of sight.
They are like a love-sick lover,
A fawning at your door.
You can tell him to go to hell,
But they keep coming back for more.
When you're walking with your darling,
People stop you and admire.
If she doesn't stop a barking.
She'll be in the funeral pyre.

# ADAPTION – A SLAM POEM

At 92, do you think I don't know about adaption.
All my fucking life I've had to adapt.
From the cradle to the grave.
Fit in, don't rock the boat.
Guess what, at 92, I can do whatever I please.
They ask me, 'Do you still drive, do you go out at night?'
'Shall we take the lift?'
Damn right we will!
Wallow in it.
I do.
I've adapted to the situation,
'Can I take your arm?'
You see, I'm used to walking in with a man.
Not much hope of that.
All the men I knew are dead.
Red watery eyes stare up at me now.
They glide smugly by in their disability scooters,
Fueled by their last drops of testosterone.

Old ladies, with irritable bowel syndrome
Wait for their sons to call.
I am a wily widow hot to trot,
I'm really as ripe as seventeen, and just as sweet.
A lover, not live in, would be dandy,
Especially if he is good-looking and handy.
Adaption, the secret of fitting in.
We are expected to live with technology.
I have acquired some passwords as I make my way through life.
They are many and they're varied and can get me in some strife.
A password to those Pearly Gates is tattooed on my breast,
Next to 'No Resuscitation', St Pete at your behest.
I've made sure it has six letters, pair of asterisks to complete.
On my entry into Paradise it should acquire a seat.
No more struggles with technology -- won't be googling anymore,
Leave my phone and my computer outside the cloudy door.
The wisdom of the centuries will make my spirit soar,
And overwhelming happiness seduce my soul once more.

# WAR GAMES

*Seen on a US army documentary*

I signed up for the military,
After all it's just a job.
I felt proud in my uniform,
I'm on the side of God.
Marching, grueling training,
They put us through the hoops.
Blazing sun or raining,
March in shiny boots.
We are ready now for combat,
They've closely shaved my head.
I've said good-bye to Mum and Dad,

To the slaughter I was led.
We piled into the aircraft,
Destination was unknown.
It didn't matter anyway,
They've consigned me to a drone.
I'm nice and cosy in my metal box,
With air-con, and Macca's with the lot!
I gaze in my computer,
It's a lousy job I've got.
I'm spying on a family
As they perform their daily tasks,
What a sneaky occupation,
Unaware today's their last!!

# THE KISS

It was wrong you know.
But so astonishingly perfect.
But wrong.

I'm suspended.
You line the inside of my eyelids.
I didn't want that.

No good will come of it, you know.
Please . . . Please
And yet!

# SILENCE

Silence is purity.
It is a soothing of the soul.
Beginning meditation,
the cluttered mind,
jumbled, chaotic,
slowly absolves itself.
It takes time, practice.
But, as if by magic,
the mind capitulates.
Surrenders.
Is this eternity?

# MOTHERS BEACH, MORNINGTON

Was it named after that fateful night in 1892?
Mothers of fifteen beautiful boys
scanned the horizon
looking for a sign, any sign,
a piece of clothing, a shoe, a cap.
The darling boys.
For one mother, it was three.
It was a disaster.
From Mordialloc to Mornington,
The fated team of footballers foundered in a storm
Never to be heard of again.
At the cliff top, a white stone memorial.
Ice cream lickers wander by, oblivious.
Mothers watch toddlers paddle in the shallows,
Blindly unaware of the history of those other mothers.

# THE ICE QUEEN

Death.
Whether if it's good or bad
depends on age and circumstance.
As the mourners troop by,
the old look serene in their Sunday best,
ready to meet their Maker.
'He was a good man,' they murmur.
Whereas,
at the one who chooses death over life,
the mourners gaze down,
baffled.
There is nothing so final as death.
No use saying,
'It was a mistake, I didn't mean it.'
We gaze down at the Ice Queen,
dressed as if going to a party.
She would have hated to grow old
Did her pearls spit and spatter in the inferno?

# TONI

She grabbed my arm,
May I walk with you?
Delicate, almost bird- like,
At 97, an extraordinary woman.
You see, I was always used to walking in with a man.
You could say, she is a magnet.
As straight as a pin with a walking stick.
She is as thin as a whippet and very smart.
All the shops know her.
The coffee shop owner sits down for a chat,
Drives her home if it is raining,
Knows her favourite cake,
Tiramisu.
Sunday lunch is a ritual at the Grand.
She sits where nobody else sits,
Goes early to avoid the crowd.
Respect is what she engenders.
Her doctor, a particular admirer,
Prescribes a morphia patch, which keeps me going.
Brings me food from his family,

Today she is going home to a pasty and her favourite cake.
Tell me about your life.
'It has been quite ordinary.
I haven't travelled, except for Canberra.
I am a farm girl, never wanted children.
Poured my love into baby lambs, goats, puppies, kittens.
No regrets there.
Worked outside in the fields, the Peninsula.
When my husband died, his friend became my lover.
He looked after me, wined, dined, and walked.
He died.
His son looks after me now. He lives in Paris, rings me every Sunday.
Visits me once a year, we dine at fancy places.
I've been in this retirement village 20 years.
Weekly hairdo, wash and set, every Thursday.
I read and stay up late, wake every day at dawn.
Until I don't.'

# THE PRIVILEGE OF AGE

My 99-year-old friend Toni
is like a piece of exquisite porcelain,
teetering on the edge.
Smart new winter jacket, pale pink,
colour-coordinated with her blouse,
We sit over our monthly lunch.
How privileged am I?
When one is 99 it seems to grant permission
for all in sundry to pause, and kiss.
'Who was that?', I ask.
'I'm not quite sure!'
Why, is it acknowledging the fact
that all cells are functioning?
My friend obliges, offering her cheek,
then concentrates on her barramundi.
The vegetables are slightly underdone.
The waitress is notified.

# ASSISTED

Toni wants to die. I want her to die.
My friend.
Trapped in her one hundred-and-two-year-old decaying body.
Cancerous sores now frame her once handsome face.
It is a daily grind, just staying alive.
The mind is as sharp as when a young girl in the army.
'Why didn't you marry the handsome pilot in the picture?'
'He was too short.'
(Poor man, I mused . . .
It didn't deter him, a rear gunner winning the Battle of Britain.)
Each week, it gets harder. I write on a pad now.
She surprises me sometimes, searching for the pen
and shakily giving a perfectly logical answer.
Today, she can hardly be bothered to respond.
It is getting harder,
But she can't let go. Neither can I.

# TO LIZZY

*by Ted Hughes, 1953*

Lizzy is so lazy, she is wee weezy,
Like a beetle in a cup,
The sides are so steep, she can't get up.
Of her laziness she sits, weep, weep.
Lizzy is better than an editor's letter,
Lizzy is softer than a feather wafter.
If Lizzy were quicker, she could trick an electric circle,
Take air by the hand, be shaplier than a thought,
And by being so be all she ought.
Lizzy is lazier than a nightwatchman's old brazier.
If Lizzy doesn't mend, I will constitute her end.

I am neither dumb nor idiot.
I am a sadder mother of both.
I have looked at you and my life is burned out.
Meaning your loveliness. Oh lady, lady.
Think me dumb, think me idiot.
I stand dumb, I know nothing that you are not.
You are lovely, speaking murders it.
You are so lovely, I have not breath,
To manage such a death before my death.
I stand mad, imagining that body,
And not another thing gets in my thoughts.

# FAMILY GATHERING

*By Daughter Jane, 3 November 2000*

Balnarring village
Friends and family rebel rousin'
Here to commemorate our Lizzy,
70 years in a tizzy.
To mark a milestone in a life.
70 years mother and wife.
Poet and comedienne,
'Run that one with me again?'
We think she missed her true vocation
When she and hubby changed location
For if our Lizzy was born again,
Her choice would be to entertain.
For Lizzy is a great Orator.
Writer, Actress, Communicator.
Whether you love her or you hate her,

She still cooks a very good Pot-at-a!
As a public speaker she has no peer,
She just says, 'Now listen here,
I'm going to read a dolly poem,'
Never mind the collective mo-an
That goes among the crowd.
The glasses are on, the voice is loud,
The audience is now enraptured,
Their imagination forcibly captured.
I wish to God, I knew her secret,
But if I know Lizzy she is going to keep it.
And hold her cards close to her chest.
She's number one, forget the rest.
So drop in friends at your will,
And hear the offerings of her quill.
Visit us when ere you will,
Just be sure not to upset Bill.

www.ingramcontent.com/pod-product-compliance
Lightning Source LLC
Chambersburg PA
CBHW071843290426
44109CB00017B/1911